20 Decorated Baskets

20 Decorated Baskets

Quick and Easy Projects to Give or Keep

Barbara S. Machtiger

Photography by Philip Stark

Martingale®
& COMPANY

20 Decorated Baskets: Quick and Easy Projects to Give or Keep
© 2003 by Barbara S. Machtiger
Photographs © 2003 by Philip Stark, NYC

This book was packaged by Barclay House Publishing
38 East 23rd Street, New York, NY 10010

Publisher and Editorial Director: Barbara S. Machtiger

Book Designer: Shelley Heller/Halcyon Endeavours
with Liz Yasuda

Project Designers: Susan Brothers, Barbara Fimbel, Shelley Heller,
Susan Hunter, Cathy O'Connor, Cheri Raymond, and Pinky Suter

Technical Editor: Cheri Raymond

Photographer: Philip Stark

Martingale & Company
20205 144th Avenue NE
Woodinville, WA 98072-8478
www.martingale-pub.com

Credits
President: Nancy J. Martin
CEO: Daniel J. Martin
Publisher: Jane Hamada
Editorial Director: Mary V. Green
Managing Editor: Tina Cook
Copy Editor: Melissa Bryan
Design Director: Stan Green

Printed in China
08 07 06 05 04 03   8 7 6 5 4 3 2 1

Library of Congress Cataloging-in-Publication Data available upon request.

ISBN: 1-56477-506-2

Mission Statement
Dedicated to providing quality products and
service to inspire creativity.

Acknowledgments

The wonderfully creative baskets that grace these pages are the work of seven very talented designers and exceptional women whose enthusiasm, commitment, and unflagging good humor made working on 20 Decorated Baskets *a sheer delight.* My deep-felt thanks to Susan Brothers, Barbara Fimbel, Shelley Heller, Susan Hunter, Cathy O'Connor, Cheri Raymond, and Pinky Suter. I hope we can do it again, soon.

To Philip, Marion, and Travis at Stark Studio, thanks for creating a serene atmosphere for the photo shoot amid the chaos of renovation. The music was perfect. To Cyrus Newitt, a special thanks for coming to our rescue at, literally, the eleventh hour.

And a personal and professional thank-you to the consummate team at Martingale & Company, each of whom, from the very start, made this experience truly a collegial collaboration.

Contents

Happy Events & Holidays

Introduction

Ever since humans set up housekeeping, people in every culture of the world have used baskets for all manner of daily chores: from catching, collecting, preparing, cooking, carrying, and serving food to cradling infants and storing goods.

Today, baskets are still favored for their humble appearance and functional nature. They continue to be made from a variety of natural materials, such as grasses and reeds, twigs and bark, split woods, bamboo, wicker and rattan, rush and rope, and palms and corn husks. But today's baskets are also constructed of man-made materials, such as plastic, metal, wire, and combinations of modern and traditional materials, which offer more choices for our contemporary lifestyles.

Baskets are everywhere, and the selection is almost as plentiful as the uses for them. Many baskets are defined by their shapes: the graceful sweep of a cut-flower basket, the compartmentalized sections of a utensil basket, the distinctive cradle shape of a baby carrier are just a few examples. Of course all baskets, regardless of individual appearance, remain ideal receptacles for toting, holding, containing, organizing, and storing items of every kind.

Because they provide easy access to their contents, baskets have become popular decorating accessories and accent pieces. And once that decorative aspect comes into play, could any craftsperson resist imbuing a simple, unadorned basket with her or his unique creative touch? Not a chance!

The projects in this book, then, should help you satisfy that urge to embellish, and hopefully will provide inspiration for your own imaginative basket designs. Employing a variety of easy craft techniques and readily available materials, these twenty decorated baskets are both pretty and practical. In a matter of hours or in a weekend, you can make one or more baskets to use around your home or to give as gifts. And if you can't find the exact size or shape of baskets shown here, don't worry. These designs are adaptable to whatever baskets you do have.

So gather the necessary supplies, find a comfortable work space, and start transforming your baskets from basic to beautiful.

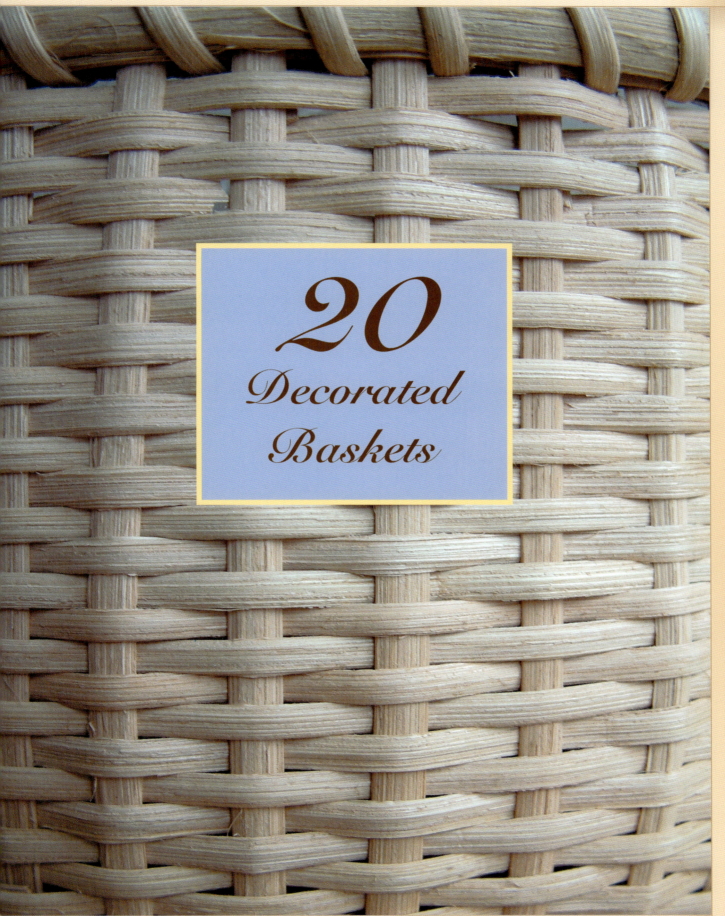

20
Decorated
Baskets

Pearly Sewing Basket

Designed by Shelley Heller

MATERIALS

Basket: Small woven-splint basket with hinged lid and movable handle (ours measures 6" deep x 8" wide x 4" high, excluding handle)

• Buttons: about 200 same-size pearly white buttons, ⅜"–½" in diameter, with 2 holes

  Assorted sizes and styles of white, pearl, red, and pink buttons

  1 ornamental red/gold button

  1 decorative clear glass button for handle

• Cherry-red enamel spray paint

• Fine sandpaper and soft cloth

• White craft glue (clear drying)

INSTRUCTIONS

1. **To paint basket,** gently sand entire basket to smooth wood, remove any splinters, and round off sharp edges. Wipe off wood dust with soft cloth. Lightly spray basket with a coat of red enamel; let dry. Repeat, applying four or five coats, letting paint dry thoroughly between coats. Paint should cover wood with a rich, glossy color.

2. **To decorate lid,** start at edge and glue a row of small two-hole buttons around basket lid, with holes facing in same direction and buttons overlapping slightly to fit. Continue gluing small buttons to make second and third rows. Do not cover hinges or seam opening, and periodically check to be sure lid opens freely.

3. Glue other white and pearl buttons of assorted sizes, overlapping, to make fourth and fifth rows, as shown in photograph.

4. Glue an overlapping arrangement of red and pink buttons to cover center of lid; finish with ornamental button in the center. Allow glue to dry overnight.

5. **To decorate sides,** glue two rows of small two-hole buttons along top rim of basket. Glue one row of identical buttons along bottom rim. If possible, try not to overlap buttons on these rows.

6. Let glue dry 24–48 hours. Glue will dry clear, letting the red paint show through the button-holes for a lacelike effect.

7. Glue decorative clear glass button to center of handle. To lift lid, glue single small two-hole button extending halfway from underside of center of lid rim. Be sure handle clears button.

Designer's Notebook

Other decorating ideas: Leave the basket natural and glue on wooden buttons for a rustic look. Or paint the basket your favorite color and decorate with tiny shells instead of buttons.

*W*hether you use this basket to store basic sewing supplies or the cache of buttons we all seem to collect, its perky cherry-red color and gaggle of glued-on pearly buttons render it too pretty to hide away.

Stars-and-Stripes Magazine Basket

Designed by Pinky Suter

Basket: Slant-top wicker magazine basket with natural (unbleached) muslin liner (ours measures 10" wide x 10" deep at base [11" at open top] x 8" high at front [9½" at back])

- 2½ yards of 2½"-wide red-and-natural stripe cotton ribbon
- 15 die-cut unpainted 1½" wooden stars
- High-gloss spray enamel: marine blue and white
- Thread to match liner
- Hot-glue gun and glue sticks
- Fine sandpaper and soft cloth
- Pencil for marking fabric
- Pinking shears
- Sewing machine
- Tape measure

INSTRUCTIONS

1. Remove liner from basket. Gently sand any rough spots on basket; wipe basket thoroughly with soft cloth to remove wood dust and any dirt.

2. Spray entire basket, inside and out, with marine blue paint; let dry. Spray two or three coats as necessary for complete coverage, letting paint dry between coats.

3. **To stitch ribbon collar to liner,** first remove any ties from liner, then measure and mark center front of liner interior. Measure and mark 1" to each side of center mark.

4. Measure and mark 10" from one end of ribbon; align this mark with 1"-from-center mark on liner. Pin ribbon to liner from inside, aligning bottom edge of ribbon with edge of liner; pin all around to other 1"-from-center mark. Machine stitch edges of ribbon to liner, beginning and ending at 1"-from-center marks. Cut ribbon 18" from end of stitching. (One end of ribbon will be 10" long; other end will be 18" long.)

5. Aligning liner and basket corners, insert liner into basket; fold ribbon collar over rim to outside of basket. Tie ends of ribbon in a large, loose, flat knot as shown in photo. Trim ends to equal length, then use pinking shears to trim into Vs.

6. **To add stars,** spray-paint wooden stars white; be sure paint covers front and sides (let dry and paint back of stars, if desired). When dry, hot-glue five stars evenly spaced to front of basket, about 1½" above bottom. Repeat on sides.

Designer's Notebook

Make multiple matching baskets of various sizes to elegantly organize a home office or to store paperbacks, videos, and CDs.

*C*ollected in this chairside basket, your favorite magazines are always at the ready for some relaxing reading. The patriotic motif fashioned of ribbon, paint, and a few wooden stars evokes a piece of folk art.

Seascape Spa Basket

Designed by Cheri Raymond

MATERIALS

Basket: Frosted plastic utility basket with rows of holes and movable metal handle (ours measures 9" square x 6½" high)

- 3 small bags of decorative flat glass marbles: dark green, light green, iridescent blue
- Assorted small seashells and 4 starfish
- Small package of natural-color raffia
- Hot-glue gun and glue sticks
- Scissors

Designer's Notebook

Be sure the marbles are large enough to cover the holes in the basket. You may find it easier to apply the hot glue around the holes, then affix the marbles.

To make a bath tote for a college student to carry supplies to and from a dorm shower room, use decorative flat marbles, craft foam shapes, acrylic gemstones, mosaic chips, or large beads in bright or school colors. Trim with colored nylon twine.

INSTRUCTIONS

1. If possible, remove metal handle from basket to make working easier. Leave top row of holes free for weaving raffia later. Working one side at a time, first hot-glue one starfish where desired, then hot-glue glass marbles over 25%–50% of the holes, arranging colors and spaces in a pleasing design. Let glue set before beginning next side.

2. Continue working as above until entire basket is decorated.

3. Separate raffia into two bunches of four or five strands each. Measure perimeter of basket rim (ours is 36"). Cut raffia to this measurement. Beginning at center front and ending at center back, weave each bunch of raffia halfway around basket rim in opposite directions. Tie ends in a casual knot or bow at the front and back. Trim raffia ends if desired.

4. Hot-glue assorted small shells along raffia; let dry. Replace metal handle if removed.

*S*porting sea-colored gems, starfish, and shells from a crafts store, this utilitarian storage basket becomes a pretty addition to the bathroom while it does its job of keeping all those pampering bath goodies organized.

Skirted Bedside Organizer

Designed by Cheri Raymond

Basket: Wicker utensil basket (ours measures 6½" wide x 12½" long x 5½" high)

- ¼ yard of your choice of fabric
- 3 yards of ready-made upholstery piping in coordinating color (upholstery piping is wider than regular piping, which can be substituted)
- 1½ yards of matching 1"-wide ribbon for bows
- Thread to match fabric
- Double-sided tape
- Dressmaker's marking pencil
- Fabric scissors
- Hot-glue gun and glue sticks
- Iron
- Sewing machine with zipper-foot attachment
- Straight pins

INSTRUCTIONS

1. **To make skirt,** measure around outside of basket (perimeter) and top to bottom (height). From fabric, cut a strip the same size as the height plus 1" (for hem) and the perimeter plus ½" (for seam allowance).

2. Stitch together short ends of skirt; press seam open. Pin piping along top edge of skirt, right sides together and raw edges matching. Allowing for a ½" overlap, cut piping to size. Using zipper foot, machine stitch piping to skirt top, sewing very close to piping; overlap ends and stitch to secure. Fold raw edges to wrong side and machine stitch just below piping on right side.

3. Temporarily tape skirt to rim of basket. Mark corners with dressmaker's pencil, then mark where bottom hem should fold; remove skirt and tape. Fold and pin hem evenly to wrong side all around; machine stitch hem with matching thread.

4. Cut ribbon into four even lengths. Fold each length of ribbon in half and pin center to corner marks on skirt; thread tack in place. Set skirt aside.

5. **To trim basket sections,** measure interior perimeter of each section; cut remaining piping to fit sections. Hot-glue piping around interior rim of each section. Tuck raw ends into a corner (a knitting needle or pencil tip helps) and hot-glue to secure.

6. **To attach skirt to basket,** slip one end of each ribbon through weave of basket at each corner. Tie ribbon ends snugly and make a neat corner bow; trim ends to form a V.

Designer's Notebook

This practical organizer can be made for use in the bathroom, nursery, family room, or home office just by selecting a fabric to complement the room's decor.

Dressed in a removable skirt to match your bedroom decor, a divided basket on the nightstand keeps loose items such as eyeglasses, lotions, reading material, and portable phone neat and close at hand.

Laundry Basket with Clothespin People

Designed by Shelley Heller

MATERIALS

MATERIALS

Basket: Oval wicker laundry basket with tie-on liner (ours measures 19" wide x 24" long x 11" high, excluding handles)

- 2 yards of 2"-wide floral ribbon or ready-made ruffle trim (measure circumference of basket liner to determine exact yardage)

- 13' of cotton clothesline

- 2 dozen round-headed wooden clothespins

- Acrylic paints in a variety of colors

- Fine-point permanent marker in black and assorted colors (optional)

- Pencils: soft lead pencil for drawing details; others to support clothespins while painting

- Clear acrylic spray sealer

- Artist's paintbrushes: small fine-tipped (eyeliner brush will work) and small flat brush

- Hot-glue gun and glue sticks

Designer's Notebook

Use new or vintage flat- or round-headed clothespins. The latter can be found at garage sales, flea markets, or on-line auction sites.

Cut pieces of felt or fabric in the shapes of petals and leaves and hot-glue them onto clothespin heads and bodies to resemble flowers.

INSTRUCTIONS

1. **To make clothespin people,** use photo on page 21 as inspiration and lightly pencil guidelines for facial features, arms, and clothing directly onto clothespins.

2. **To paint bodies and clothes,** wedge a pencil between legs of clothespin to hold it securely for painting. Paint heads and upper bodies in a variety of skin colors; let dry. Paint variety of hair colors and styles; let dry. Paint clothes and shoes; remove from pencil to paint inside legs. Let dry completely.

3. **To paint faces,** return clothespins to pencil. Use fine-tipped brush with paint, or permanent markers, to draw facial features, arms, and accessories.

4. When all clothespin people are finished and paints are dry, spray all with two coats of acrylic sealer, letting dry between coats.

5. **To trim basket liner,** cut floral ribbon or ruffle trim in half. Remove liner from basket. Hot-glue one length of ribbon to wrong side of front section of liner, overlapping edge by ¼". In the same way, glue remaining length to back section. Insert liner back into basket, and tie.

6. **To finger-crochet clothesline chain,** thread one end of rope around handle as shown (fig. 1); leaving 9" free, lightly tie to handle. Holding long end of rope in left hand, form 1" loop between thumb

*W*ho says doing the laundry has to be dull? The whimsical chain gang of
hand-painted clothespin people hanging around this ordinary laundry basket
is sure to make even laundryphobes look forward to wash day.

and forefinger. With thumb and forefinger of right hand, reach through loop, grasp rope and pull through, forming a new loop (fig. 2). As you pull second loop through first, allow first loop to tighten (fig. 3). Repeat to make third loop.

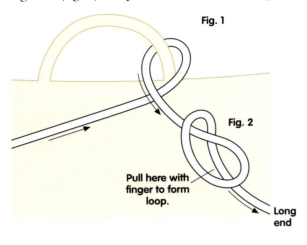

Fig. 1

Fig. 2

Pull here with finger to form loop.

Long end

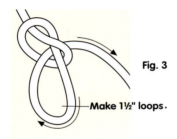

Fig. 3

Make 1½" loops.

7. Continue in the same manner, chaining loops about 1½" long, until chain is long enough to reach other basket handle.

8. **To loop across handle,** thread loose end of rope under and around handle from front, then–pull taut and across to opposite side of handle (fig. 4). Loop over and around handle, pull cord taut, begin chain.

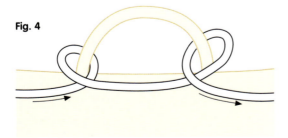

Fig. 4

9. **To finger-crochet clothesline chain along other side of basket,** repeat steps 6 and 7, chaining to first handle. Loop rope around handle, pull taut (fig. 5).

Fig. 5

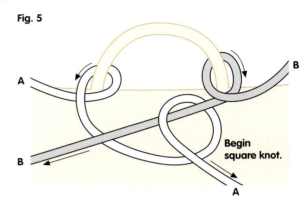

A

B

B

A

Begin square knot.

10. **To finish rope chain,** tie rope ends together in a square knot across handle (fig. 6). Cut rope ends long enough to tuck into loops on handle.

Making a Square Knot

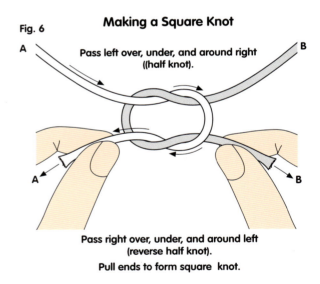

Fig. 6

A

B

Pass left over, under, and around right ((half knot).

A

B

Pass right over, under, and around left (reverse half knot).

Pull ends to form square knot.

11. Turn chains over. Starting at center loop of chain, insert a clothespin person. Continue inserting clothespin people on each side of first one, one per loop, twelve per side. Position clothespin people so feet are standing among flowers on lining trim. Repeat on other side of basket.

Three-Tiered Hanging Baskets

Designed by Susan Brothers

MATERIALS

Baskets: Set of 3 hanging wire baskets in graduating sizes (ours are copper and measure 8", 10", and 12" in diameter)

- 2 garlands of silk pothos or other mid-size vine, each about 9' long

- 1 garland of silk boxwood or other small-size vine, about 8' long

- 1 yard of 2½"-wide yellow wire-edged ribbon

- Assorted warm-colored silk flowers (sunflowers, dahlias, asters)

- 32-gauge green cloth-covered wire

- Hot-glue gun and glue sticks

- Wire cutters

INSTRUCTIONS

Note: It's easier to work on the individual baskets if you disassemble the baskets and chains and then reassemble them to complete the decorating.

1. Using wire cutters, cut cloth-covered wire into 4" lengths (approximately 40) to fasten garlands to baskets and chains.

2. **To trim basket rims,** begin with small basket and wire the end of one pothos garland to a basket rib where it joins the rim. Continue to wire garland at intervals until entire rim is covered. Overlap ends 1"; clip with wire cutters.

Repeat, wiring remainder of first pothos garland to rims of medium and large baskets.

3. **To trim hanging chains,** lay chains flat and, beginning at top of one chain, wire the end of second pothos garland to chain link. Continue wiring garland down chain at 2" intervals. Using wire cutters, clip garland 1½" below end of chain. Repeat, wiring garland down remaining chains.

4. **Reassemble baskets and chains.** Tuck extended vine at end of each chain into rim of basket below. Hang basket to finish decorating.

5. Beginning at bottom basket, weave boxwood garland randomly through basket ribs, up a chain, and around other baskets' ribs and chains, ending at hook at top chain.

6. Position flowers in a pleasing arrangement on baskets' rims and chains; hot-glue in place.

7. Make a double bow with yellow ribbon (see Gingham Baby Carrier, page 46). Wire bow to hook at top of chains; trim ends into a **V**.

Designer's Notebook

For a pretty showerside basket, substitute ivy, flowers, and a bow to complement the colors of the bathroom. Use as a holder for soaps, sponges, brushes, and bath gels.

*C*limbing vines and sunny flowers twining around a copper hanging-basket ensemble will add a cheery touch to a dull corner of your kitchen. The baskets can provide a holding place for produce or dried herbs and spices.

Stenciled Wine Caddy

Designed by Pinky Suter

Basket: Double wine caddy with flat sides of metal, wood, or wide woven slats (ours is metal, measuring 8" wide x 5¼" high, excluding handle)

- Two 9" x 12" sheets of clear acetate
- Acrylic paints: white, medium green, dark green, purple
- Acrylic matte medium
- Matte-gold spray paint
- Clear acrylic spray sealer
- Fine-point permanent black marker
- Craft knife with very sharp, fine blade
- Mineral spirits or fine sandpaper and soft rag (see step 1)
- Masking tape
- Mixing palette
- Self-healing cutting mat
- Small artist's paintbrush

INSTRUCTIONS

1. If using a metal caddy, wipe with rag dampened with mineral spirits to remove any dirt or grease. If using a caddy made of wood or woven slats, gently smooth surface with sandpaper and wipe with soft rag to remove wood dust.

2. Spray entire caddy gold. Set aside to dry.

3. **To properly size stencil design,** measure front, back, and sides of caddy to make sure stencil motifs (page 26) fit. Leaves–and–grapes motif should fit on front and back; two–leaves–and–tendril motif should fit sides. Leave a margin of ⅜" from edge at top and ends of motifs. Enlarge or reduce stencil motifs on a photocopier as necessary to fit your basket. On final photocopied stencil, draw a horizontal registration line ⅜" above vines.

Note: You will need to make and cut out three separate stencils: 1) leaves, vine, and tendrils; 2) grapes; and 3) two–leaves–and–tendril motif.

4. **To prepare stencils,** align top edge of acetate sheet with registration line on photocopy, taping edges to keep acetate from moving. With fine-point permanent marker trace entire grapevine design. Draw horizontal line 1" below tracing, cut across on line, label as stencil 1. Repeat to make and label stencil 2. In the same manner, trace two–leaves–and–tendril motif and label as stencil 3.

5. **To cut stencils,** always draw cutting knife into shape that will be removed to avoid accidental cuts. Place stencil 1 on cutting mat and, using craft knife, carefully cut out vine, tendrils, and interior grape leaves only (leaf ribs are not cut out); set aside. Place stencil 2 on cutting mat and carefully cut out grape stems and grape bunches only; set aside. Place stencil 3 on cutting mat and cut out all parts; set aside.

A grapevine is an apt motif to decorate a wine caddy, and stenciling is an easy way to create it. This technique calls for applying and blending paint colors with an artist's brush rather than dabbing them on with a stencil brush.

6. **To paint stencil motifs,** align and center top edge of stencil 1 at top rim of caddy; tape in position. In mixing palette, blend together small amount of medium green paint, drop of white, and bit of matte medium to form consistency of thick cream. Using artist's brush and small amounts of paint, carefully brush paint in from edges of stencil, leaving leaf ribs and veins un-painted. Use dark green to outline veins of leaves, then blend dark into lighter green of leaves.

7. Using dark green paint, outline lower edges of vine and tendrils, blending dark into lighter green across stencil. Let paint dry. Remove stencil, clean with damp paper towel, let dry. Repeat steps 6 and 7 on opposite side of caddy.

8. Align and tape stencil 3 to one end of caddy. Using same colors and techniques as in steps 6 and 7, paint one end of caddy, then repeat on opposite end.

9. Align and tape stencil 2 to front of caddy. In mixing palette, blend together small amount of purple paint, drop of white, and bit of matte medium to form consistency of thick cream. To give grapes dimension, brush paint in from one edge of all grapes in a cluster, then blend purple into the lighter purple in each grape cluster. Let paint dry before removing stencil and repeating on opposite side of caddy.

10. When paint on caddy is thoroughly dry, spray entire caddy with clear acrylic sealer.

Front and Back

Stencils are actual size.

Sides

Pet Bed with Storage Drawer

Designed by Cheri Raymond

*P*amper your pet with a custom-made bed that has a drawer underneath for toys, brushes, and grooming tools. The size shown is suitable for pets up to 20 pounds, but the instructions can be adapted to any size basket.

MATERIALS

Baskets: Shallow rectangular wicker basket with cut-out hand grips for bed (ours measures 16" wide x 21" long x 6" high); divided rectangular wicker utensil basket to fit under bed (ours measures 12" wide x 15½" long x 2¾" high)

Note: Consider height and width of legs (see below) when purchasing drawer basket, to enable drawer to move smoothly in and out

- 1½ yards of 45"-wide fabric of choice for mattress cover and drawer trim

- 1 yard of furniture batting (used for upholstery padding, it's about 2" thick and much firmer than quilt batting), cut into 2 pieces to fit the length and width of bed interior (for the size shown, batting was cut 14" wide x 19" long)

- 4 large, round wooden screw-in curtain-rod finials for legs

- 1 wooden-knob drawer pull to match legs

- 4 non-skid self-adhesive pads for bottom of legs (optional)

- Die-cut wooden bone (dog) or fish (cat) for nameplate

- Non-toxic acrylic paints and flat paintbrush

- Hot-glue gun and glue sticks

- Iron

- Sewing machine and thread to match fabric

INSTRUCTIONS

1. Cut one 1½"-wide strip across width of fabric. Cut two fabric rectangles 3" longer and 3" wider than cut batting (for the size shown, fabric was cut 17" wide x 22" long). Fold and press long edges of fabric strip ¼" to back.

2. **To make bed,** screw four finial legs into bottom corners of bed basket. Hot-glue legs in place from interior of bed. Affix self-adhesive pads to bottom of legs, if desired, to prevent sliding on hardwood, vinyl, or tile floors.

3. **To make drawer,** hot-glue wooden knob to center front of utensil basket. Hot-glue fabric strip over rim of basket to form bindinglike trim.

4. **To make mattress cover,** machine stitch fabric rectangles right sides together, using ¼" seam allowance and leaving 8" opening for turning.

5. **To make box corners for mattress,** press edge seams open, separate layers at corners, then fold to match seams in center as shown in illustration below. Stitch 3" seam across corner perpendicular to center seam. Trim excess to make ¼" seam allowance. Repeat with all four corners. Turn cover right side out through opening.

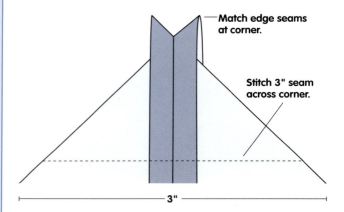

Making a Box Corner

6. Layer the two pieces of furniture batting to form mattress. Roll up mattress lengthwise and stuff into mattress cover through opening. Unroll and smooth to fill mattress cover and fit into corners. Slipstitch opening closed.

7. **To form "corded" edges of mattress,** hand stitch all around mattress top about ½" from edges. Repeat stitching around mattress bottom. Place mattress in bed.

8. **To make nameplate,** paint die-cut wooden bone or fish in desired color; hand letter pet's name. Hot-glue to front of basket.

Cozy Knitting Basket

Designed by Shelley Heller

*E*very needleperson needs a basket for the current project-in-progress.
This one features a lining and accessory pockets of felt, the
perfect fabric complement to the softness of yarn.

INSTRUCTIONS

Note: It's unlikely that you'll find a basket with the exact dimensions or shape as the one shown. Therefore, adjust the length of the collar and pockets to fit your basket.

1. **To make patterns for basket liner,** measure circumference of basket at widest part; measure height. Using marker, draw rectangular pattern of these dimensions on kraft paper; label pattern "side lining." Outline basket bottom on kraft paper; label pattern "bottom lining." Cut out patterns.

2. **To make lining,** pin patterns to lining felt. Cut out lining pieces, adding a ¼" seam allowance.

3. Place side lining inside basket and pin darts to shape to fit interior. Remove lining and baste side seam. Pin bottom lining to lower edge of side lining. Place lining inside basket, adjust pins so bottom fits; remove and baste bottom seam and side darts. Using ¼" seam allowance, machine stitch side seam; trim excess. Machine stitch darts and bottom seam; trim.

4. **To make collar pattern and collar,** measure basket rim from handle base to opposite base of same handle on one side of basket; this is length of one-half of collar. With marker draw a rectangle on kraft paper 4" high x length of half-collar; label pattern "collar" and cut out. Pin pattern to collar/pocket felt. Cut out felt half-collar ¼" from edge of pattern to allow for seam allowance. Repeat to make second half-collar.

5. **To make slits in collar for weaving ribbon,** fold one collar piece in half lengthwise. With fold on bottom, use marker to lightly draw a line ¼" above fold and ¼" below edge; lightly draw a 1½" vertical line 1" in from each end. Beginning on end line and ¼" bottom line, mark an even number of 1½" vertical slits equidistant across collar (slits as shown are 1½" apart). Cut slits with fabric scissors, through one layer of felt only, cutting last slit on opposite end line (see illustration below). Trim ends of collar with pinking shears. Measure, mark, and cut second collar piece.

Cutting Collar Slits

Fold at bottom

6. **To make pocket pattern and pocket,** measure the short distance along rim between the two handles; this is width of pocket. Determine length of pocket by measuring distance from rim to 1½" from bottom of basket; double this measurement. Using marker, draw a rectangle on kraft paper the width of pocket x doubled length; cut out pattern. Pin pattern to collar/pocket felt. Cut out felt pocket piece; pink long edges. Repeat to make second pocket piece.

7. **To cut curved edge of pocket front,** lay out one pocket. Measure and mark halfway down the strip (for later placement of curved pocket edge). On each side edge, measure up and mark 2¼" from bottom of strip. In center, measure up and mark 2½" from bottom of strip (see pocket illustration). Using pinking shears, cut a gentle curve between these marks. In same manner, measure, mark, and cut second pocket piece.

8. **To cut pocket front snowflake design,** fold curved pocket edge up to halfway mark made in step 7. Mark the fold; this section with the curved edge is the pocket front. Fold this section into quarters. Holding folds tightly and using sharp scissors, cut out tiny triangles on quarter folds to make snowflake design; unfold and press. Cut out a scrap of lining felt the same size and shape as pocket front. Place behind snowflake and thread tack. In same manner, cut and line second pocket.

9. Fold curved edge of pocket front up to halfway mark, snowflake facing you. Machine stitch seams of pocket ⅛" from edge on both sides.

10. **To sew collars and pockets to basket lining,** insert lining into basket, seam side against basket. Fold one collar piece in half lengthwise, place inside lining, slits facing lining. Align top edges; pin together from handle base to handle base. In same manner, pin second collar piece to lining on opposite side. Pin pockets to lining, snowflake facing lining, between handles on opposite sides of basket. Remove lining and baste rim seam all around; remove pins. Machine-stitch rim seam, attaching collars and pockets to lining. Trim any excess felt at seam allowance.

11. Placing lining in basket, adjust collars and pockets to align properly with handles. Fold collars and pockets over rim to outside of basket.

12. **To finish,** beginning at basket front, weave ribbon through slits in collar all around basket. Tie bow in front. Fold bow tails into a V on wrong side of ribbon; glue or thread tack to hold in place. Tie embroidery scissors to end of satin cord, tie other end of cord to basket handle. Tuck scissors into pocket.

Making Pocket

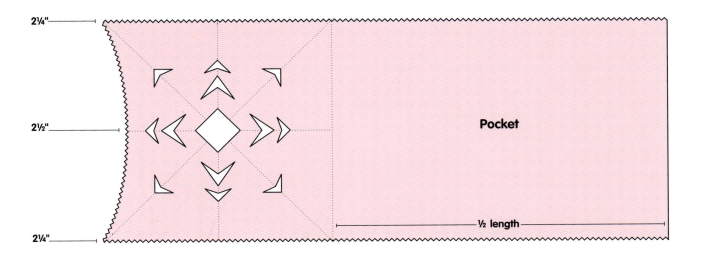

Fold and cut snowflake design into 1 layer of felt.

Gardening Basket with Tool Pockets

Designed by Pinky Suter

MATERIALS

Basket: Large wicker gardening basket (ours measures 15" wide x 29" long x 7" high, excluding handle)

- ½ yard of plaid vinyl mesh fabric (outdoor-furniture fabric or vinyl-coated cotton tablecloth fabric can be substituted)

- 5 yards of 1"-wide and ⅓ yard of ¼"-wide grosgrain ribbon to complement fabric

- Thread to coordinate with plaid fabric and ribbon

- Medium green high-gloss spray enamel

- Dark green acrylic paint

- Acrylic gloss medium

- High-gloss clear acrylic spray sealer

- 1"-wide bristle paintbrush

- Scissors, both paper and fabric

- Paper towels

- Sewing machine

- Straight pins

- Utility brush and soft cloth

INSTRUCTIONS

1. With a stiff utility brush and soft cloth, thoroughly clean basket of any dust, dirt, or grease.

2. Spray entire basket, inside and out, with medium green paint; let dry. Apply two or three coats as necessary for complete coverage, letting paint dry between coats.

3. Mix dark green paint with gloss medium to consistency of heavy cream; paint should be evenly dark but translucent. Brush onto basket, covering about nine square inches at a time. With crumpled paper towel, lightly blot paint from surface of wicker, creating weathered look. Continue painting and blotting a section at a time to weather entire surface of basket; let dry overnight. Spray basket inside and out with acrylic sealer.

4. **To make tool pockets,** measure width and length to best fit your basket (the ones shown are approximately 8½" x 13"). If necessary, enlarge or reduce pattern on photocopier to fit these measurements. Pin pocket front and pocket back patterns to vinyl fabric; cut out two of each. Mark positions of loops with pins.

5. **To make pocket loops,** cut ¼"-wide ribbon into four 2½"-long pieces; turn ends under ¼" twice and stitch to prevent raveling. Sew two loops to each pocket back where pin-marked, adjusting placement as necessary to align loops with basket handles.

A classic cut-flower garden basket gets a pretty makeover with paint and removable vinyl tool pockets. A great helpmate for the dedicated gardener, it also makes a perfect gift, perhaps filled with packets of heirloom seeds.

6. **To bind top edges of pockets,** cut four pieces of 1"-wide ribbon the same length as top edge of pocket front and back pieces; fold ribbons in half lengthwise. Place folded ribbons to sandwich raw edge of each pocket piece; machine stitch through all layers to bind.

7. **To assemble pockets,** lay out pocket back, right side up, and lay pocket front on top of it, also right side up. Machine stitch down center of pocket front to create two compartments. In same manner assemble second pocket, omitting center seam, if desired.

8. **To bind pocket edges,** cut two pieces of 1"-wide ribbon the same length as raw edge of pocket; fold ribbons in half lengthwise. Place one folded ribbon to sandwich raw edge of pocket. Machine stitch around pocket edge, easing around corners and turning ends under to prevent raveling. Repeat to bind second pocket.

9. Cut remaining 1"-wide ribbon into four pieces about 18" long; thread through pocket loops and tie pockets to basket handles with bows. Trim bow tails and cut into Vs.

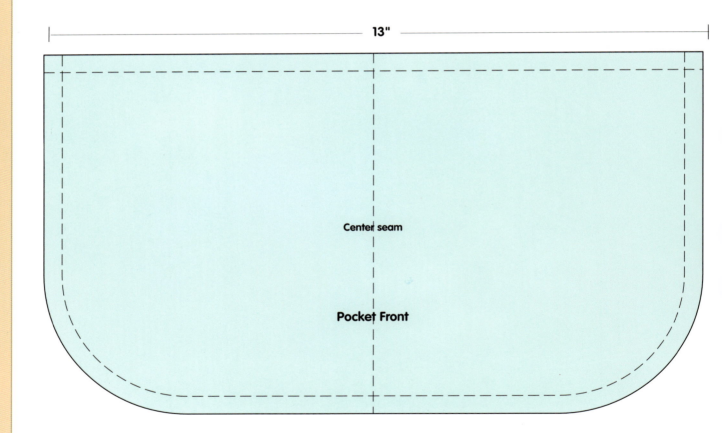

13"

Center seam

Pocket Front

Enlarge pattern 200% for size of basket shown or proportionately to fit your basket and garden tools.

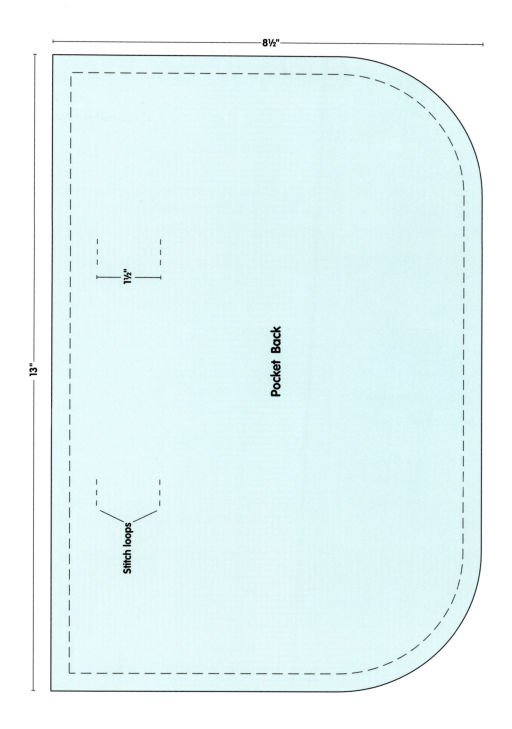

8½"

13"

1½"

Pocket Back

Stitch loops

**Enlarge pattern 200%
for size of basket shown or
proportionately to fit your
basket and garden tools.**

Nantucket Bridal Basket

Designed by Cheri Raymond

MATERIALS

Basket: Large Nantucket lightship–style basket with handle, or finely woven basket with wooden base and handle (ours measures 12½" in diameter x 6" high, excluding handle)

- 1 yard of pale blue silk (or color of choice) for lining

- 2½ yards of 1"-wide lavender-blue wired ribbon

- 4–5 sprays of silk lily-of-the-valley

- 3–4 sprays of silk lavender or speedwell (or flower of choice)

- White matboard, cut 10" square (or size necessary to duplicate shape of wooden base)

- Tracing and transfer papers and pencil

- Craft or utility knife

- Hot-glue gun and glue sticks

- Iron

INSTRUCTIONS

1. **To cut basket lining,** measure around interior basket rim (circumference) and inside from center bottom to the top edge (depth). Cut a strip of lining fabric to fit depth and circumference plus ½" seam allowance. Stitch together short ends of lining strip. Press seam allowance open. Fold ½" along top edge of lining to wrong side; press.

2. **To line basket,** hot-glue folded edge of lining just under the inside rim, gluing first one spot and then its opposite (12 o'clock—6 o'clock; 9 o'clock—3 o'clock, and so on around rim) to position lining evenly around basket. In the same manner, hot-glue lining along bottom edge of basket, pleating fabric as necessary for a smooth fit. Trim bottom lining 1" from glued edge (raw edges will be covered by base panel).

3. **To make the interior base panel,** outline wooden bottom of basket onto tracing paper. Place transfer paper on matboard and center tracing on top; outline over tracing to transfer shape. Cut out. Lay matboard on wrong side of remaining lining fabric. Cut fabric 1" larger than matboard all around. Fold fabric over opposite edges of matboard all around, hot-gluing to secure as you work.

4. Hot-glue base panel to bottom of basket interior, being sure to cover raw edges of lining.

Lucky is the summer bride who passes out party favors from this lovely Nantucket-style basket. To show off its refined weave, it is decorated simply with lily-of-the-valley, lavender, and ribbon, and lined in matching azure silk.

5. **To decorate outside of basket,** begin at one end of handle and hot-glue sprays of lily-of-the-valley and lavender along outside rim on both sides of basket, ending about 3" from opposite end of handle. You may wish to cut stems shorter before gluing.

6. **To decorate handle,** hot-glue sprays of lily-of-the-valley and lavender along half of handle.

7. Cut ribbon into lengths of 1 yard and 1½ yards. Fold longer ribbon in half widthwise; hot-glue fold to center top of handle, hiding glued portion under flowers. Crisscross ribbon halves evenly down handle, wrapping around flower stems to hide glue; knot to secure, leaving streamers.

8. Make bow from remaining ribbon. Tie securely to handle with streamers. Clip all ribbon ends to form a V.

9. Hot-glue extra leaves to radiate from bow along handle and basket rim as shown in photo. Adjust shape of bow as desired.

Interior of lined bridal basket.

Designer's Notebook

Hydrangea, freesia, apple blossoms, violets, daisies, and ivy would all be lovely on this basket. Keep it fresh and simple to complement the elegant basket weave. For a winter wedding or engagement party, entwine winter berries or holly with ivy. Fill the basket with individually wrapped gingerbread men for your holiday guests.

This basket would also be ideal to collect the "shower of wishes" notes and cards given to the bride-to-be at her bridal shower.

Flower Girl's Basket

Designed by Shelley Heller

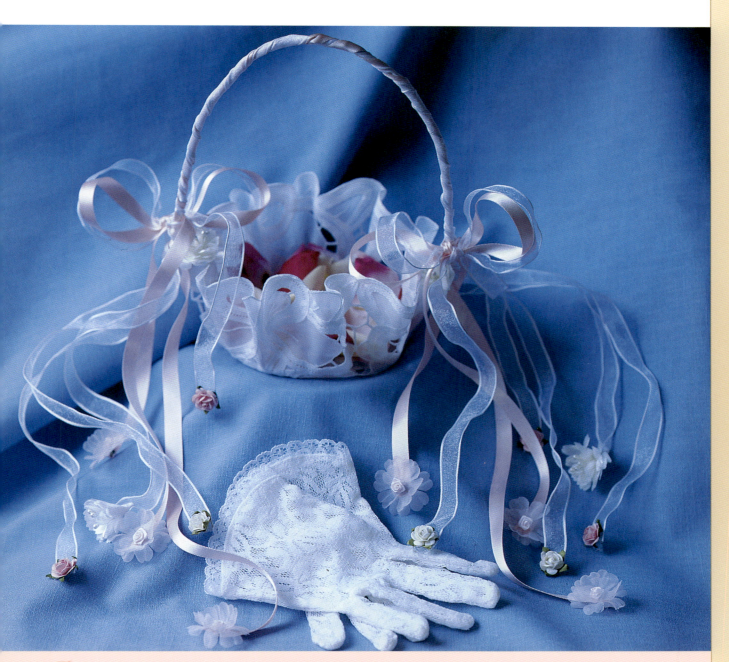

*P*icture a special little girl in her first fancy dress, strewing petals from this delicate lace-doily basket as she precedes the bride down the aisle. Just a few simple materials will create a future family heirloom.

- 10"-diameter Battenberg lace doily
- 6½ yards of ¼"-wide white sheer wire-edged ribbon
- 3½ yards of ¼"-wide pink satin ribbon
- Approximately 16–20 assorted small pink and white silk flowers
- Hot-glue gun and glue sticks
- Bowl with 4½"-diameter flat bottom
- Small bottle of fabric stiffener and bowl for soaking doily
- White wire coat hanger
- Wire cutters and needle-nose pliers

Designer's Notebook

Make a doily basket for candy or to put on a dresser to hold jewelry and trinkets by eliminating the handle.

Individual nut or petit four cups to set beside each place setting at a dinner party can be made by draping 5" doilies over the bottom of an overturned juice glass or small jar. Before putting unwrapped food in the doily cups, cut circles of parchment paper and place one on the bottom of each cup to absorb any grease.

To make a bridal favor basket, use an 18" doily and form the basket over a large bowl. Fill with small gifts for wedding guests.

INSTRUCTIONS

1. **To form basket,** thoroughly soak doily in bowl of fabric stiffener, following manufacturer's directions. Turn flat-bottom bowl upside down on work surface protected with a towel. Center wet doily over base of bowl, letting edges drape down over sides. Using fingers, form soft pleats evenly spaced around sides, creating basket shape. Let dry 24 hours. Gently remove dried basket from bowl.

2. **To make basket handle,** use wire cutters to cut off 16"-long bottom of coat hanger. Shape handle by bending this wire over bowl used to form basket. With needle-nose pliers bend up both ends of wire to form ½" hooks. Hot-glue these hooks between inside folds of pleats on opposite sides of basket. Hot-glue a flower to basket at base of handle on each side.

3. From pink ribbon cut one 54" length. From white ribbon cut three 54" lengths. Layer ribbons on each other; beginning 8"–9" from end of ribbons, hot-glue them to handle base. Wrap ribbons around handle wire, hot-gluing as needed. Hot-glue ribbon ends to opposite handle base, leaving streamers.

4. **To make handle bows,** cut two pink and two white ribbons 36" long. Using one pink and one white ribbon, tie a bow at each handle base; hot-glue to secure.

5. Trim ribbon streamers from handle and bows to varying lengths. Hot-glue white and pink flowers to the ends of streamers.

6. Fill basket with flower petals just before sending flower girl down the aisle.

New Home Welcome Basket

Designed by Cathy O'Connor

Got a new neighbor, or a friend who moved into a new home? Show your creative side by presenting this whimsical backyard-in-a-basket. Add some seedlings or seed packets for a unique housewarming gift.

MATERIALS

Basket: Shallow rectangular basket (ours measures 8½" wide x 13" long x 3" high, exclusive of handles)

- 4' of 4¼"-high picket fencing for crafting
- Acrylic craft paints: white, red, black, and colors of choice for birdhouse and sign
- 2 bags of dried reindeer moss
- Tiny red and yellow dried cluster flowers (e.g., statice)
- Slightly larger dried flowers for clay pots
- 2 small clay flowerpots (¾"–1" high)
- 1½" x 3" piece of balsa wood or die-cut wooden signboard
- Die-cut wooden banner (3½"–4")
- Miniature birdhouse on pole (10"–11")
- 2 miniature birds (½"–1")
- Miniature table and chairs painted white
- Artist's paintbrushes: flat and fine-pointed
- Hot-glue gun and glue sticks
- Small craft saw or sturdy craft or utility knife
- Tweezer

INSTRUCTIONS

1. Paint fencing white on both sides, covering wood completely; let dry. Paint inside band and handles of basket white, if applicable (your basket may not have a band or handles).

2. **To make fence,** cut fencing into sections measuring the same as basket sides. To make front gate section, cut a 2"-wide piece out of center of one long side of basket. Cut a 2"-wide piece from center of one long fence section (for gate).

3. Hot-glue small bunches of moss to cover entire outside of basket. Hot-glue fence sections to basket sides over moss. Hot-glue gate to front in open position as shown in photo. Touch up with white paint as necessary.

4. Cut small bunches of tiny dried flowers with their stems from the main flower. Put a small drop of hot glue on each little flower stem and adhere to moss between pickets along crossbar at fence bottom to give the appearance of flowers growing out from behind the fence. Alternate and mix flower colors for a natural look.

5. **To make flagstone path,** measure depth and width of pickets on each side of gate opening. On opposite corners of balsa wood, cut right angle to fit pickets. Mix a bit of black and white paint to make gray, and paint balsa wood; let dry. Mix some red and white paint to make pink. Using photo for reference, paint irregular-shaped pink and white flagstones on path as shown; let dry. Outline flagstones with fine black line; let dry.

6. **To mount path** at gate opening, hot-glue path to bottom of pickets at fence opening, hiding cut angles under moss. Add more moss if necessary.

7. Glue moss into flowerpots; glue larger flowers into moss. Hot-glue flowerpots to flagstone path on each side of gate opening as shown.

8. Paint birdhouse and pole as desired; let dry. Hot-glue a bit of moss to birdhouse opening; hot-glue bird to perch. Set aside.

9. **To make welcome sign,** paint wooden banner as desired; let dry. In pencil, lightly hand letter the word *Welcome* onto banner. Letter over pencil with paint; let dry. Hot-glue a flower to each side of banner. Hot-glue banner to top of pickets at gate opening. Hot-glue remaining bird to top of sign.

10. **To line basket,** hot-glue moss inside basket, covering entire bottom and sides, leaving white basket rim exposed, if applicable. Glue moss above basket rim from inside; glue small bunches of flowers to moss between pickets along crossbar at fence top.

11. Insert birdhouse pole through moss, into weave, at basket bottom on "lawn" behind left front fence. Hot-glue pole securely to basket from underneath.

12. Use tweezer to pick off glue threads from basket. Arrange miniature furniture in "backyard."

Designer's Notebook

This design can be easily adapted to welcome a sweet new baby, using softer colors for flowers, the baby's name over the gate, and tucking in a stack of washcloths, diaper pins, lotions, soaps, or other necessities for the newborn. Or present this basket as a birthday gift with the recipient's name on the sign and a miniature cake on the table.

Hot-gluing tips:
To prevent burning your fingers when using a hot-glue gun, consider wearing rubber fingers—the kind used for gripping and sorting papers. They're available at most stationery stores.

To avoid the little threads of glue that occur from using a glue gun, you can make a hot-glue "dip tank" by melting several glue sticks in an old electric frying pan or in an old saucepan heated on an electric hot plate. Dip the flower ends into the melted glue and adhere them to the basket as directed.

Gingham Baby Carrier

Designed by Susan Hunter

Basket: Rush baby carrier (also called a Moses basket; ours measures 18" wide x 30" long x 9" high, excluding handles)

- 4 yards of lavender checked gingham or baby print of choice
- 1 yard of white cotton fabric
- 4 yards of 2"-wide gathered white lace trim
- 8 yards of 1"-wide white moiré ribbon
- 6 yards of 2½"-wide wire-edged lavender moiré ribbon
- ¼" thick foamboard, approximately 20" x 30"
- Batting, cut same size as foamboard
- 26-gauge craft wire, cut into four 6" lengths
- Craft or utility knife
- Hot-glue gun and glue sticks
- Spray adhesive
- High-tack tape (optional)
- Iron and ironing board

INSTRUCTIONS

1. From lavender gingham, cut a 12"-wide strip across length of fabric to make flounce; set aside. To make lining, measure interior of basket and cut another strip to fit basket depth plus 2" and circumference plus 1".

2. **To line basket,** begin inside basket at midback and position lining around sides of basket, folding top edge of fabric over rim by about ½"; hot-glue to outside of basket. Fold short end of lining under ½" and finger-press; hot-glue over starting end. Smooth lining down inside basket and hot-glue lower edge along bottom of basket.

3. **To make the baseboard,** spray adhesive on one side of foamboard; align and adhere batting to board. Turn foamboard over, center basket bottom on board, and outline lightly in pencil. Using craft knife, cut out foamboard/batting along outline. Trim as necessary so that baseboard will fit inside basket.

4. Place baseboard, batting side down, on white fabric; cut fabric 1" larger all around. Fold fabric over opposite edges of board 1" at a time and hot-glue to secure. Repeat, folding and gluing opposite edges around back of baseboard. (You may want to tape down for added security.) Turn baseboard fabric side up and place in basket.

5. **To make flounce,** place 12"-wide gingham strip wrong side up on ironing board. Fold top edge down 5½" along length of strip (bottom layer will extend 1" below folded length); press. Fold up bottom extension ½"; fold up ½" again, over 5½" layer; press. Hot-glue layers together along entire length. Hot-glue gathered edge of lace trim along this to finish bottom of flounce.

*I*s there a mother-to-be who wouldn't love to receive this precious baby carrier as a shower gift? And believe it or not, the ensemble is made without using one single stitch! It's all done with the magic of a glue gun.

6. **To pleat and attach flounce**, begin at midback outside rim of basket and run a 2"-long bead of hot glue over previously glued edge of lining; adhere top edge of flounce. Form a pleat by pinching 2" of top edge of flounce into a 1"-deep fold. Anchor pleat with dot of hot glue on basket just in front of pleat; finger-press in place. Run a 4"-long bead of hot glue along rim to adhere more flounce fabric; make another pleat and anchor (see illustration below). Continue gluing and pleating every 4" around rim until you reach starting point. Trim flounce length if necessary. Fold raw edge under and hot-glue end to meet first pleat.

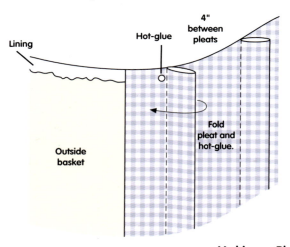

Making a Pleat

7. Measure circumference of basket rim. Cut white ribbon to that length plus 2" for overlap. Beginning at midback of flounce top, hot-glue ribbon over glued pleats, folding back each pleat as shown in photo. Overlap and hot-glue ribbon ends to finish.

8. **To make bows,** cut wire-edged ribbon into four 1½-yard lengths. Using one length for each bow, leave a tail of about 6" and, with long working end of ribbon, make a loop about 3"; pinch at end of loop. Bring working end of ribbon forward into another 3" loop and pinch both loops together at center forming a bow. Repeat to make another bow on top of first. Make a small loop in center of double bow and pinch

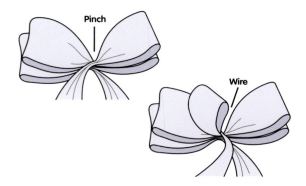

Making a Double Bow

(see bow illustration). Twist a 6" piece of floral wire around center of bow, fastening loops together tightly. Manipulate wire to back of bow and trim ends.

9. Separate bow loops and fluff into shape. Cut bow tails into a V. Hot-glue bow to rim at center front of basket. Repeat, making three more bows for back and sides; hot-glue in place.

10. **To make white streamers and tails,** cut remaining white ribbon into eight streamers, each 13½" long, and eight tails, each 9" long. Using photo as guide, hot-glue one streamer between large loops on each side of bow; drape up and hot-glue to white ribbon along rim of basket. Hot-glue two tails under center loop of each bow. Cut streamer and tail ends into Vs.

Designer's Notebook

If the baby carrier is going to get lots of use in the months ahead, it would be a good idea to sew the ensemble to make it more secure. The lining can be hot-glued as instructed, then thread tacked in spots to be sure it holds. Then place a purchased baby-carrier mattress pad and bumper ensemble inside.

Ribbon-Weave Heart Box

Designed by Pinky Suter

This Cinderella-like transformation of a humble heart-shaped wire box into an exquisite token of love is achieved by ribbon weaving, a simple technique that can be done on any open-weave basket or box.

Basket: Heart-shaped open-weave wire basket with lid (ours measures 10½" wide x 10" long x 3" high)

Note: It's unlikely you'll find a wire basket that's exactly the same dimensions and weave pattern as the one shown. Therefore, use the materials list as a guide only and experiment weaving ribbon patterns and designs on your basket with scraps of ribbon to achieve a pleasing and balanced appearance before purchasing the amount of ribbon you'll actually need.

- 30 yards of ½"-wide pink satin ribbon, or color of choice
- 1 yard of lightweight batting
- 1 yard of lining fabric in color to match ribbon
- Nosegay of ribbon or silk flowers
- Lightweight posterboard, large enough to line basket sides
- Matboard, large enough to outline basket base 3 times
- Several sheets of plain white paper to make heart patterns
- Hot-glue gun and glue sticks
- Large plastic yarn needle (optional, for ribbon weaving)
- Needle and thread to match ribbon (optional)
- Spray adhesive

INSTRUCTIONS

1. **To make patterns for basket linings,** outline basket lid and base onto white paper, draw a cutting line ¼" inside outlines, cut out, and label patterns "lid" and "base." Set aside until step 4. For side lining, cut a full–length strip of lightweight posterboard to the height of the basket interior minus ¼". (Large baskets may need two strips of posterboard taped together to get lining length.) Fit this strip snugly around basket interior to determine correct length; trim to length. Set aside until step 6.

2. **Weave basket lid** in desired pattern (see Note). For basket shown, the entire top of lid was woven with a continuous ribbon and a yarn needle, weaving first on the diagonal in one direction, then wrapping rim (whipstitching) to reverse direction, and repeating until top was completely woven. Side of lid was not woven.

3. **Weave sides of basket** in desired pattern (see Note). For basket shown, individual ribbon strips were cut, one end was folded over upper rim, thread tacked, and then woven diagonally down side. Opposite ends of ribbon strips were folded to underside of basket and thread tacked to wire frame as needed for support. These ribbon ends on bottom (see detail photo on facing page) will be sandwiched between base lining and covered bottom piece. Ribbon ends on interior will be covered by side lining.

4. **To make covered basket bottom and padded lid and basket base linings,** outline one lid and two base lining patterns (see step 1) onto matboard; label and cut out. Spray adhesive onto matboard lid and one matboard base piece; adhere to batting. Let adhesive dry and cut out along matboard edges.

5. Lay matboard lid and base pieces batting side down on wrong side of lining fabric. Cut out fabric 1" from matboard edge. Clip lining fabric close to matboard at V cleft of heart. Fold fabric to back of matboard lid and hot-glue all around. Repeat to make one padded base lining. Cover remaining unpadded matboard base piece with lining fabric in same manner.

6. **To make padded side lining,** spray adhesive on back of posterboard side lining strip (see step 1); adhere to batting. Let adhesive dry and cut out along posterboard edge. Lay posterboard strip batting side down on wrong side of lining fabric. Cut out fabric ¾" from posterboard edge. Fold fabric to back at short ends of posterboard and hot-glue. Fold fabric over top and bottom edges; hot-glue to posterboard.

7. **To assemble basket base,** use small dots of hot glue to adhere padded side lining strip inside basket, beginning and ending at bottom point of heart to hide seam.

8. Insert padded base lining to fit snugly on basket bottom. Turn basket over; dot hot glue along base lining edge through wire weave. Align unpadded fabric-covered base piece to underside of basket, sandwiching all ribbon loose ends between. Press inside and outside pieces together while glue sets. Base lining and base bottom will be bonded together through wire weave.

9. **To assemble basket lid,** dot hot-glue along inside edge; insert padded lid lining to fit snugly. Press inside while glue sets.

10. Attach floral nosegay to lid with small stitches or dots of hot glue.

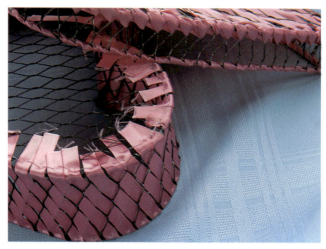

Underside of basket before lining and base cover are added.

Ribbon flowers are arranged to lay flat on lid and thread tacked in place.

Designer's Notebook

If you'd like to make your own ribbon flowers, consult any number of ribboncraft books found at your favorite bookstore or online.

Floral Easter Basket

Designed by Cathy O'Connor

MATERIALS

Basket: Round white-painted willow basket with rigid handle (ours measures 8" in diameter x 5" high, excluding handle)

- 12–15 stems of silk flower clusters: 2 sizes or types, in different shades of one color
- 24" lengths of ¼"-wide ribbons: 2 sheer, 1 satin, in 3 shades of same color
- Hot-glue gun and glue sticks

Designer's Notebook

Purchase more flowers than you think you'll need, in case some become damaged or you decide to change the design.

If the flower stems have buds in addition to flowers, glue them around the rim in place of opened flowers.

Change the look of the basket by using different color or flower combinations: roses in shades of pinks and reds, pansies in a mix of colors, a variety of yellow flowers, or daisies combined with violets, for example.

INSTRUCTIONS

1. Cut individual flowers and leaves from stems. This basket was made with 1½" purple flowers (about 90) and 1" lavender flowers (about 110). Arrange flowers into two piles according to color or size, to make it easier to select alternate flowers as you work.

2. Beginning at basket rim and alternating flower color/size, hot-glue flowers close together around rim.

3. Repeat, working in rows around basket. Depending on style of basket, you may wish to leave 1"–2" of basket showing at base. When basket is covered with flowers, glue a few leaves randomly between them around basket.

4. Hot-glue end of each ribbon to base of handle on one side. Holding ribbons together, wrap them as one around handle, keeping the spirals parallel as shown. Hot-glue ribbons along underside of handle to keep them in place. Glue ends securely at opposite base of handle. Trim excess ribbon.

5. Hot-glue a small flower to cover ends of ribbons at bases of handle. Hot-glue a small cluster of flowers and leaves near top of handle, slightly off center.

A blanket of purple and lavender silk flowers envelopes a white willow basket roomy enough to hold the Easter Bunny's stash of holiday eggs or a leafy green spring plant.

Mother's Day Trinket Box

Designed by Barbara Fimbel

Basket: Round cane basket (or other flat-weave basket) with hinged lid and metal latch (ours measures 8" in diameter x 5" high)

- Variety of print images in desired theme (make multiple color photocopies to have lots of choices)

- 3 yards of ¼"-wide decorative metallic gold paper edging

- 1 yard of rhinestone trim

- Tassel in color to coordinate with images

- Decoupage medium (preferably one that is both glue and sealer) and 1"-wide foam brush

- 2 pairs of fine-point paper scissors for detailed cutting: one with straight blades and one with curved blades

- Hot-glue gun and glue sticks

Designer's Notebook

Consider the interests of the person receiving the basket and the occasion when deciding what motifs to use for decoupaging. A few suggestions:

White doves and flowers for a bridal shower

Plants, birds, and garden tools for the gardener

Maps, old travel postcards, and foreign stamps for a bon-voyage gift

INSTRUCTIONS

1. Cut out a large selection of images to allow plenty of choice.

2. **To decorate,** lay out images for lid directly on basket; for sides, arrange images on flat work surface. When you're pleased with arrangements, begin to decoupage lid: Working one small area at a time, remove an image, brush lid with decoupage medium, brush back of image with medium, and adhere image to lid. Continue until lid is completed, then in same manner, decoupage images around sides. When entire basket is covered to your liking, apply a coat of decoupage medium over all. Allow to dry thoroughly.

3. Brush decoupage medium on back of gold edging and adhere around top and sides of lid and around top and bottom of basket as shown in photo. Trim edging as necessary to fit around clasp and hinges. Brush edging with medium and allow to dry thoroughly.

4. **To seal and protect,** apply two or three coats of decoupage medium, allowing each to dry thoroughly before reapplying.

5. **To finish,** hot-glue rhinestone trim around top rim as shown. Attach tassel to latch.

The ornate motifs of Victorian greeting cards were the inspiration for this decoupaged box. A simple cut-and-paste technique on a round lidded cane basket results in an elegant gift for the best mother in the world.

Spooky Halloween Party Baskets

Designed by Cathy O'Connor

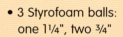

MATERIALS

Skeleton

Basket: Small round willow basket with handle (ours measures 5" in diameter x 3" high, excluding handle)

- 3 Styrofoam balls: one 1¼", two ¾"

- White enamel spray paint

- Acrylic craft paint: red, black, orange, white

- Brush-on crystal glitter paint

- Blue-violet glitter dust

- Crimped white paper shreds and clear iridescent decorative grass

- Plastic drinking straw, cut 3" long

- 2 red sequins

- 2 straight pins with white ball heads

- 1 cup flour plus 1 cup water

- Newspaper cut into strips 1" x 5" and 2" x 4"

- ¾"-wide transparent tape

- Artist's paintbrushes: flat, round, and pointed

- Hot-glue gun and glue sticks

- Mixing bowl & whisk

- Craft or utility knife; wire cutters (optional)

INSTRUCTIONS

1. **To make mouth,** cut slits ¼" apart along width of straw. Bend cut straw into a smile shape and hot-glue to front of basket.

2. **To make cheeks,** cut 1¼" foam ball in half; hot-glue halves to front of basket on each side of mouth.

3. **To make papier-mâché,** mix flour and water together in mixing bowl, stirring with whisk to form paste of smooth, thick, workable consistency. Dip 1"-wide newspaper strips into paste one by one, and layer diagonally on basket, covering cheeks and mouth. Use wet fingers or flat wet paintbrush to smooth paper. Continue until entire basket is covered with papier-mâché. If desired, papier-mâché inside of basket.

4. **For each eye socket,** place one 2" x 4" strip of newspaper on a flat surface; using flat brush dipped in papier-mâché paste, saturate paper. Fold strip in half lengthwise, then bring ends together to form socket, making sure that ¾" foam ball fits into socket. Attach sockets to basket with small pieces of newspaper dipped in papier-mâché paste. Keep smoothing with wet fingers and/or brush. Let dry overnight.

5. Spray basket inside and out with white enamel, making sure paint covers all nooks and crannies. Let dry thoroughly. Paint red rims on eye sockets, a black triangle nose, and an orange mouth. When mouth is dry, paint white and black teeth.

*S*imple techniques and a variety of easy-to-use craft supplies will keep little goblins happy helping to create these kooky, spooky party baskets. One made from a larger basket would be great for trick-or-treating.

6. Hot-glue foam eyeballs into sockets. Thread a sequin onto each straight pin and insert into center of eyes. If pins protrude inside basket, cut them with wire cutters. Paint red veins on eyeballs.

7. **To finish basket body,** brush crystal glitter paint onto basket. While still wet, sprinkle on blue-violet glitter dust. Repeat on handle.

8. **To make hair,** adhere pieces of crimped paper and iridescent grass along one edge of 2" lengths of tape. Fold other edge over to secure grasses. Hot-glue tape around inside rim of basket until hair is full.

MATERIALS

Spider

Basket: Small round willow basket with handle (ours measures 5" in diameter x 3" high, excluding handle)

- Black enamel spray paint
- Brush-on crystal glitter paint
- Metallic black glitter
- Pipe cleaners: 1 green 12" straight chenille, 8 black 12" tufted chenille stems
- ¾" Styrofoam ball
- Beads: 2 orange pony beads, 2 smaller white beads
- Artist's flat paintbrush
- Craft or utility knife
- Hot-glue gun and glue sticks

INSTRUCTIONS

1. Spray basket inside and out with black enamel paint; let dry.

2. Brush on crystal glitter paint. While still wet, sprinkle on metallic black glitter. Repeat on handle.

3. **To make pinchers,** cut green pipe cleaner in half. About ½" from bottom of basket, insert pipe-cleaner halves 1½" apart in center front, through space in weave; hot-glue to inside. Trim ends to 1½" and curl inward.

4. **To make eyes,** cut foam ball in half; paint black. Let dry. Brush crystal glitter paint onto flat side. While still wet, sprinkle on metallic black glitter. When dry, hot-glue to basket above pinchers, flat side facing out.

5. Hot-glue white bead to orange bead. Hot-glue beads to eyes.

6. **To make legs,** cut four tufted chenille stems to make long legs as shown, leaving three tufts and a narrow stem at each end. Cut four shorter legs, leaving two tufts and a narrow stem at each end. Bend legs as shown.

7. Alternating short and long legs on each side, insert narrow stem end of each leg through basket weave and bend upward inside. Hot-glue to inside of basket.

MATERIALS

Cat

Basket: Small round willow basket with handle (ours measures 5" in diameter x 3" high, excluding handle)

- Black enamel spray paint
- Brush-on crystal glitter paint
- Blue-violet glitter dust
- $\frac{1}{16}$"-thick craft foam: yellow, orange, black, white
- 12" white pipe cleaner
- Tracing and transfer papers and pencil
- Artist's flat paintbrush
- Craft or utility knife
- Hot-glue gun and glue sticks

INSTRUCTIONS

1. Spray basket inside and out with black enamel paint; let dry.

2. **To make foam shapes,** trace templates for ears, eyes, nose, mouth, teeth, and moon onto tracing paper. Place transfer paper over appropriate colored foam and place tracing over transfer paper. Outline tracings. Remove papers and cut out foam shapes.

3. Using photo for reference, hot-glue orange inner ears to black ears; glue ears inside rim of basket, next to handle. Glue yellow eyeballs to orange rims; glue black iris in center of yellow eyes. Glue orange nose and eyes to basket. Glue four white teeth to orange mouth; glue to basket.

4. **To make whiskers,** cut pipe cleaner into 2" lengths. Dab end of each whisker with crystal glitter paint. While still wet, sprinkle with blue-violet glitter dust. Insert opposite end of three whiskers through basket behind each corner of mouth. Hot-glue ends to inside of basket.

5. Brush crystal glitter paint onto yellow foam crescent moon. While still wet, sprinkle with blue-violet glitter dust; let dry. Hot-glue to handle as shown.

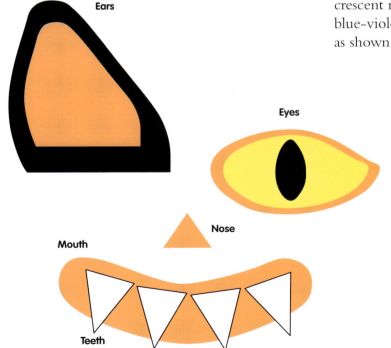

Ears

Eyes

Nose

Mouth

Teeth

Moon

Templates are actual size.

MATERIALS

Bat

Basket: Small round willow basket with handle (ours measures 5" in diameter x 3" high, excluding handle)

- Black enamel spray paint and orange acrylic craft paint
- Brush-on crystal glitter paint
- Metallic glitter: black and copper
- 1/16"-thick craft foam: 9" x 12" sheet of black and scrap of white
- 3 black 12" bumpy chenille stem pipe cleaners
- 3/4" Styrofoam ball
- 2 stick-on wiggle eyes, 15mm
- 24-gauge floral wire, cut in 8", 10", and 12" lengths
- Tracing and light-colored transfer papers and pencil
- Artist's flat paintbrush
- Craft or utility knife
- Hot-glue gun and glue sticks

INSTRUCTIONS

1. Spray basket inside and out with black enamel paint; let dry. Brush on crystal glitter paint. While still wet, sprinkle on metallic black glitter. Repeat on handle.

2. **To make foam shapes,** trace wing, teeth, and bat templates from facing page onto tracing paper. Place transfer paper over black foam and place tracings over transfer paper. Outline tracings of wing and bat. Make two wings and three bats. Remove papers and cut out foam shapes. Repeat with white foam to make two teeth.

3. **To edge wings,** begin at rounded end of wings and hot-glue pipe cleaner along top. Trim, leaving 1" extension to join wings to basket. Reserve remaining pieces of pipe cleaner.

4. **To make eyes,** cut foam ball in half; paint orange. Let dry. Hot-glue flat end to basket, about 1/2" below rim. Brush on crystal glitter paint. While still wet, sprinkle metallic copper glitter; let dry. Attach wiggle eyes.

5. Cut tufted areas from remaining pipe cleaner and reserved pieces. Hot-glue two tufts around top of eyes to form eyebrows.

6. **Hot-glue foam teeth** to front of basket as shown.

7. **To finish wings,** brush wings with crystal glitter paint. While still wet, sprinkle on metallic black glitter to cover; let dry. Insert extending 1" of pipe cleaner on wings into basket at base of handle on both sides.

8. **To make antennae,** insert two tufted pieces of pipe cleaner into rim of basket above outer edge of eyebrows.

9. **To make flying bats,** spray floral wire pieces with black enamel paint; let dry. Curl wires by wrapping them around pencil.

10. Hot-glue cut-foam bats to one end of wires. Brush bats on both sides with crystal glitter paint. While still wet, sprinkle with metallic black glitter to cover; let dry. Insert free end of wires into back of basket and bend up; hot-glue to secure.

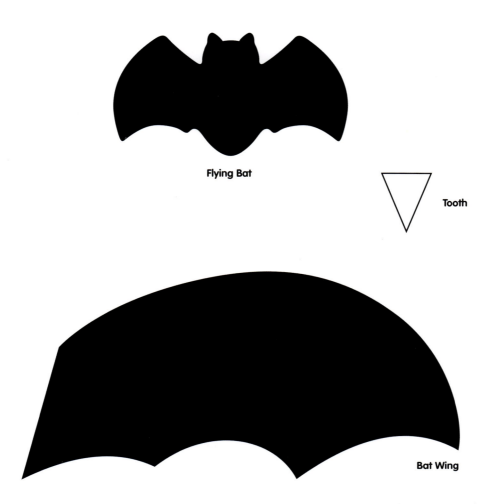

Flying Bat

Tooth

Bat Wing

Templates are actual size.

Designer's Notebook

When spray-painting the baskets, use disposable rubber gloves. Work outside or in a well-ventilated room. Protect your work surface by covering it with newspaper or a large plastic bag.

When making the skeleton basket, keep a wet rag nearby—the papier-mâché will make your hands sticky and less flexible.

A Styrofoam egg carton makes a good paint palette. The sections are perfect for holding and mixing small amounts of paint.

To prevent glitter from getting all over everything work over an empty box large enough to hold a basket with room to spare for working. This will also allow you to keep and reuse excess glitter.

Cornucopia Centerpiece

Designed by Susan Brothers

MATERIALS

Basket: Cornucopia basket with braided rim (ours measures 12" at widest point x 22" long)

- Assorted fresh and/or artificial gourds and autumn fruits and vegetables
- Nuts in the shell: walnuts, chestnuts, pecans, etc.
- 12–18 stalks of dried or silk wheat
- Dried ears of Indian corn
- Dried seedpods (e.g., lotus, beech, chestnut)
- Assorted silk or preserved maple and oak leaves
- Small artificial berries: red on green wire and orange on brown wire (about 80 each)
- 2 blocks of floral foam
- Artist's flat paintbrushes: ¼"–½"
- Craft glue, hot-glue gun, and glue sticks
- Craft paint: gold and silver
- Scissors, wire cutters, utility knife

INSTRUCTIONS

1. **To gild cornucopia basket,** nuts, and seedpods, paint entire braided rim of basket with gold paint; lightly brush paint over basket body to highlight weave. Paint nuts gold; add gold highlights to one or two larger lightweight vegetables. Paint seedpods silver. Set aside to dry.

2. **To decorate basket surface,** begin by inserting wires of red berries into weave of basket rim. Secure berries with a drop of craft glue; let dry. In the same manner, scatter red and orange berries throughout weave of basket body; glue in place.

3. Glue maple and oak leaves onto the basket surface to achieve a windblown look.

4. **To fill basket,** begin by shaping one block of floral foam with utility knife to fill narrow end of horn; be sure foam fits securely, then hot-glue in place. Arrange sprays of leaves and stalks of wheat in bottom of basket and spilling out from lower rim. Insert stems into floral foam, hot-gluing to secure if necessary.

5. Shape second block of floral foam to form a base inside basket, making hollows to support gourds and fruit. Hot-glue to bottom of basket.

6. Build a "tower" of produce inside basket opening by placing heaviest gourds, fruits, and vegetables on bottom, in foam hollows; hot-glue in place. Continue arranging and hot-gluing produce, using progressively smaller and lighter-weight items, until entire mouth of basket is filled.

7. Insert some leaves and wheat stalks at sides and near top of basket. Hot-glue gold nuts and silver seedpods into small spaces. Place extra harvest items on table, seemingly spilling from basket's mouth.

Nothing says autumn like a horn of plenty overflowing with harvest bounty. When planning this lush centerpiece for your holiday table, buy extra fruits, vegetables, berries, gourds, and nuts to make a voluptuous display.

Sparkling Christmas Planter

Designed by Shelley Heller

INSTRUCTIONS

Note: It's a good idea to work out the placement of the Christmas balls before actually gluing them on. To figure out the total number of balls you'll need, determine how many you'll need for each row and multiply by the number of rows there will be. Have extras in case some break.

1. Lightly sand basket rim to create a smooth surface. Wipe off wood dust with soft cloth.

2. Spray entire basket, inside and out, with silver paint. Apply two or three coats to rim for complete coverage, allowing paint to dry thoroughly between each coat.

3. Carefully remove and discard any metal hooks, caps, and/or wires from Christmas balls.

4. **To make first row of balls,** apply a dab of hot glue to basket just under rim; press one silver ball into place, sideways, angling neck against basket. Hold until glue is set. Continue gluing silver balls around basket, hiding neck of previous ball with next ball, until row is completed.

5. **To make second and subsequent rows:** As in step 4, glue a row of red balls, snugly fitting each red ball below and between two silver balls in row above, as shown in photo. Before hot-gluing balls in place, apply a dot of hot glue to each ball so it can adhere to row above.

6. Continue hot-gluing alternating rows of red and silver balls in place. If rows do not meet completely in back, adjust placement of balls slightly to make the gap less noticeable.

7. Place holiday plant in basket. Surround with candles to maximize sparkle, if desired.

Designer's Notebook

Take the finished basket to the florist and try out different plants to get the best effect. Look for the proper balance of proportions between plant and planter.

If the planter is for a small evergreen or cypress tree, consider decorating the tree with the same, but smaller, ball ornaments.

*A*glow *in its simple elegance, this dazzling ornament-enrobed basket is the perfect receptacle for a festive poinsettia or small evergreen that will grace a hall table or sideboard. It's glue-gun quick and makes a unique holiday gift.*

new and bestselling titles from

America's Best-Loved Craft & Hobby Books®

America's Best-Loved Quilt Books®

NEW RELEASES
1000 Great Quilt Blocks
Basically Brilliant Knits
Bright Quilts from Down Under
Christmas Delights
Creative Machine Stitching
Crochet for Tots
Crocheted Aran Sweaters
Cutting Corners
Everyday Embellishments
Folk Art Friends
Garden Party
Hocus Pocus!
Just Can't Cut It!
Quilter's Home: Winter, The
Sweet and Simple Baby Quilts
Time to Quilt
Today's Crochet
Traditional Quilts to Paper Piece

APPLIQUÉ
Appliquilt in the Cabin
Artful Album Quilts
Artful Appliqué
Blossoms in Winter
Color-Blend Appliqué
Sunbonnet Sue All through the Year

BABY QUILTS
Easy Paper-Pieced Baby Quilts
Even More Quilts for Baby
More Quilts for Baby
Play Quilts
Quilted Nursery, The
Quilts for Baby

HOLIDAY QUILTS & CRAFTS
Christmas Cats and Dogs
Creepy Crafty Halloween
Handcrafted Christmas, A
Make Room for Christmas Quilts
Welcome to the North Pole

HOME DECORATING
Decorated Kitchen, The
Decorated Porch, The
Dresden Fan
Gracing the Table
Make Room for Quilts
Quilts for Mantels and More
Sweet Dreams

LEARNING TO QUILT
101 Fabulous Rotary-Cut Quilts
Beyond the Blocks
Casual Quilter, The
Feathers That Fly
Joy of Quilting, The
Simple Joys of Quilting, The
Your First Quilt Book (or it should be!)

PAPER PIECING
40 Bright and Bold Paper-Pieced Blocks
50 Fabulous Paper-Pieced Stars
For the Birds
Quilter's Ark, A
Rich Traditions
Split-Diamond Dazzlers

ROTARY CUTTING
365 Quilt Blocks a Year Perpetual Calendar
Around the Block Again
Around the Block with Judy Hopkins
Fat Quarter Quilts
More Fat Quarter Quilts
Stack the Deck!
Triangle Tricks
Triangle-Free Quilts

SCRAP QUILTS
Nickel Quilts
Scrap Frenzy
Scrappy Duos
Spectacular Scraps
Strips and Strings
Successful Scrap Quilts

TOPICS IN QUILTMAKING
American Stenciled Quilts
Americana Quilts
Batik Beauties
Bed and Breakfast Quilts
Fabulous Quilts from Favorite Patterns
Frayed-Edge Fun
Patriotic Little Quilts
Reversible Quilts

CRAFTS
ABCs of Making Teddy Bears, The
Blissful Bath, The
Handcrafted Frames
Handcrafted Garden Accents
Handprint Quilts
Painted Chairs
Painted Whimsies

KNITTING & CROCHET
365 Knitting Stitches a Year Perpetual Calendar
Clever Knits
Crochet for Babies and Toddlers
Crocheted Sweaters
Knitted Sweaters for Every Season
Knitted Throws and More
Knitter's Book of Finishing Techniques,
Knitter's Template, A
More Paintbox Knits
Paintbox Knits
Too Cute! Cotton Knits for Toddlers
Treasury of Rowan Knits, A
Ultimate Knitter's Guide, The

Our books are available at bookstores and your favorite craft, fabric, and yarn retailers. If you don't see the title you're looking for, visit us at
www.martingale-pub.com or contact us at:

1-800-426-3126

International: 1-425-483-3313

Fax: 1-425-486-7596

Email: info@martingale-pub.com

For more information and a full list of our titles, visit our Web site.